STEM CAREERS

COMPUTER PROGRAMMER

by R.J. Bailey

Ideas for Parents and Teachers

Pogo Books let children practice reading informational text while introducing them to nonfiction features such as headings, labels, sidebars, maps, and diagrams, as well as a table of contents, glossary, and index.

Carefully leveled text with a strong photo match offers early fluent readers the support they need to succeed.

Before Reading

• "Walk" through the book and point out the various nonfiction features. Ask the student what purpose each feature serves.

• Look at the glossary together. Read and discuss the words.

Read the Book

• Have the child read the book independently.

• Invite him or her to list questions that arise from reading.

After Reading

• Discuss the child's questions. Talk about how he or she might find answers to those questions.

• Prompt the child to think more. Ask: Do you know anyone who works as a computer programmer? What projects has he or she been involved in? Do you have any interest in this kind of work?

Pogo Books are published by Jump!
5357 Penn Avenue South
Minneapolis, MN 55419
www.jumplibrary.com

Library of Congress Cataloging-in-Publication Data

Names: Bailey, R.J., author.
Title: Computer programmer / by R.J. Bailey.
Description: Pogo books edition. | Minneapolis, MN: Jump!, [2019] | Series: Stem careers | Includes index.
Audience: Ages 7-10.
Identifiers: LCCN 2018016038 (print)
LCCN 2018016782 (ebook)
ISBN 9781641281799 (ebook)
ISBN 9781641281782 (hardcover: alk. paper)
Subjects: LCSH: Computer programming–Vocational guidance–Juvenile literature.
Classification: LCC QA76.25 (ebook)
LCC QA76.25 .B325 2019 (print) | DDC 005.1023–dc23
LC record available at https://lccn.loc.gov/2018016038

Editors: Jenna Trnka and Susanne Bushman
Designer: Michelle Sonnek

Photo Credits: piotr_pabijan/Shutterstock, cover; Africa Studio/Shutterstock, 1, 23 (screen); LightField Studios/Shutterstock, 3; ANURAK PONGPATIMET/Shutterstock, 4; Andrey_Popov/Shutterstock, 5, 9, 12-13; Denys Prykhodov/Shutterstock, 6-7; iMoved Studio/Shutterstock, 8 (computer); Rawpixel.com/Shutterstock, 8 (screen); mirtmirt/Shutterstock, 10-11 (computer); fatmawati achmad zaenuri/Shutterstock, 10-11 (screen); Marcos Mesa Sam Wordley/Shutterstock, 14-15; stockfour/Shutterstock, 16-17; Indiapicture/Age Fotostock, 18; xefstock/iStock, 19; Daisy Daisy/Shutterstock, 20-21; Picsfive/Shutterstock, 23 (tablet).

Printed in the United States of America at Corporate Graphics in North Mankato, Minnesota.

TABLE OF CONTENTS

CHAPTER 1

TALKING TO COMPUTERS

Do you like computers? Do you like solving problems? You could be a computer programmer!

Computers make our lives easier. But they don't work without people. Or programs. People write **software programs** to make computers work. Who are these people? Computer programmers.

software program

We need software programs. These are instructions. They tell computers what to do. They are how a **GPS** knows the way home. They are why smartphones can do so much.

CHAPTER 2
WHAT DO THEY DO?

Programmers write **code**. This is a set of instructions. It brings software to life!

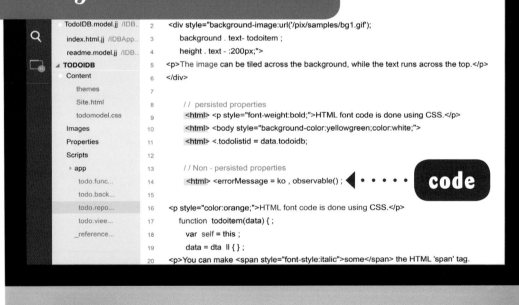

Software programs are why video games have real-life **graphics**.

Programmers use **programming languages** to write code. There are many. **Java** is one. It is popular for making **mobile applications**. This is the software on smartphones. People use **HTML** to make web pages.

```
public class HelloWorld {

    public static void main(String[] args) {
        // Print text to anything you want ...
    System.out.println("Hello, World");
    System.out.println("I want to learn java");
    System.out.println("programming language");
    System.out.println("its good");
    System.out.println("robust");
    System.out.println("and free");

    }

}
```

Java

TAKE A LOOK!

• •

HTML uses tags. The tags tell the program how to display the words, pictures, and graphics on a web page. Take a look!

HTML CODE

	`<html>`
	`<head>`
heading	`<title>Why I like to ride my bike</title>`
	`</head>`
	`<body>`
paragraph	`<p>The three reasons I like to ride my bike:</p>`
	`<ul>`
	`<li>I get exercise.</li>`
list	`<li>I like going fast!</li>`
	`<li>I like to be outside.</li>`
	`</ul>`
	`</body>` ◀ • • • • **tag**
	`</html>`

DISPLAY

heading	Why I like to ride my bike
paragraph	The three reasons I like to ride my bike:
list	• I get exercise. • I like going fast! • I like to be outside.

Minneapolis
cloudy

15°
H: 17°
L: 9°

4:23

Search

GUI ·····▶

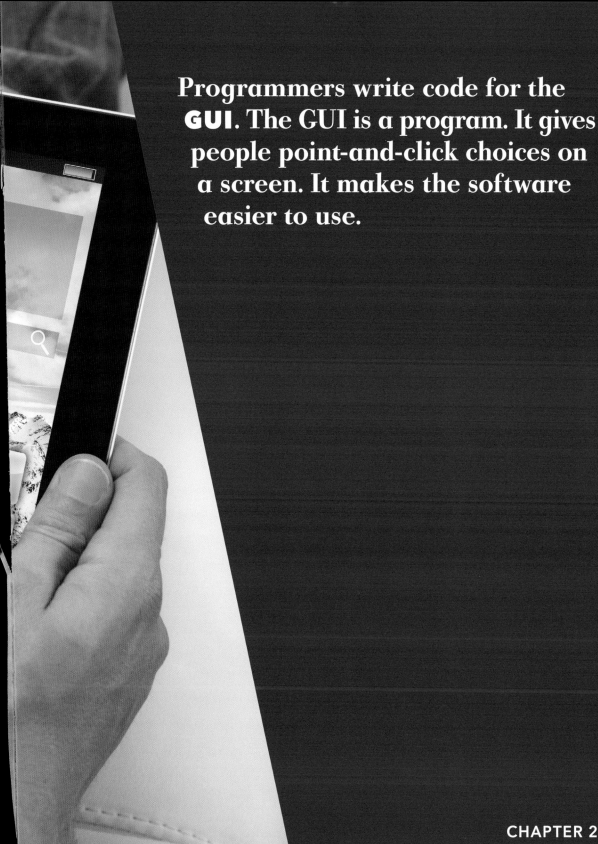

Programmers write code for the **GUI**. The GUI is a program. It gives people point-and-click choices on a screen. It makes the software easier to use.

A program can have problems. Or "bugs." They keep it from working properly. Programmers review the code. They find the bugs. They make changes. They test it. They do this until they fix the bug.

DID YOU KNOW?

Grace Hopper was a programmer. In 1947, she was working on a computer. She found a moth in it. She called it the first case of a computer bug!

Programmers work in offices. They spend a lot of time on computers. They have good concentration skills. They have an eye for detail. They often work long hours to fix bugs. Sometimes they work with other programmers.

DID YOU KNOW?

Special software tools are used for big jobs. Some tools **automate** coding. This frees up time. Programmers can write other parts of a program.

CHAPTER 3

BECOMING A PROGRAMMER

Do you want to be a programmer? Work on puzzles. They will help you learn problem-solving skills. Take computer classes. Study math.

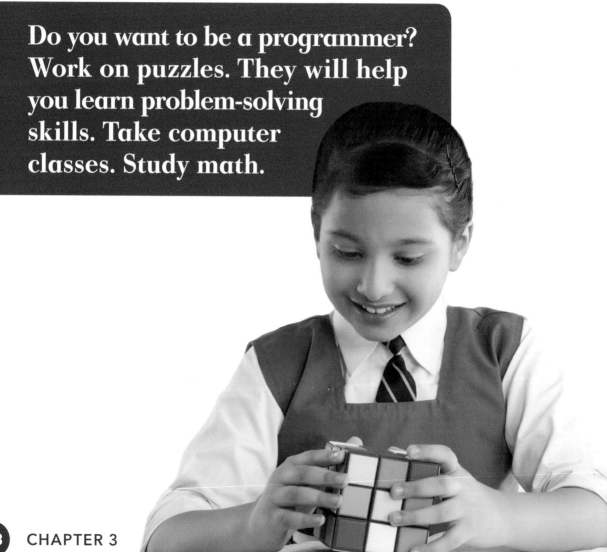

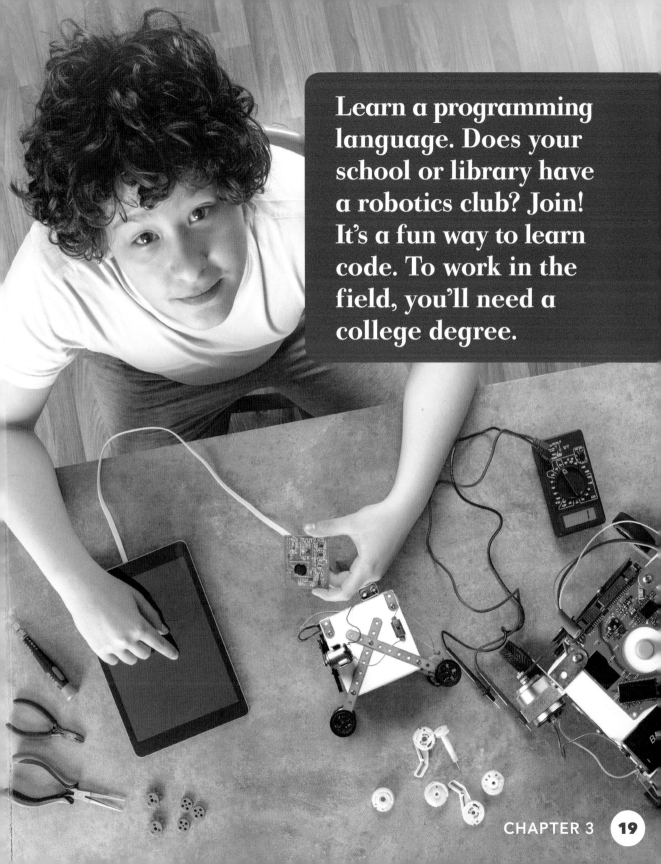

Learn a programming language. Does your school or library have a robotics club? Join! It's a fun way to learn code. To work in the field, you'll need a college degree.

As a programmer, you can shape the future. How? You can program new machines to use less **energy**. You can write programs for space travel. You can program lifesaving medical tools. The possibilities are endless!

DID YOU KNOW?

To work as a programmer, you need STEM skills. What does STEM stand for? Science. Technology. Engineering. Math. STEM careers are in demand. They pay well, too.

ACTIVITIES & TOOLS

PRACTICE WRITING CODE

Computer programmers are good at breaking down a task into small steps. In this activity, pretend you are teaching a robot to make a sandwich.

Gather the ingredients for your favorite sandwich. Then, as you make the sandwich, write the steps you take so the robot can make the sandwich without making a mistake.

When you are done, number each step in order. Your instructions are like computer code!

Review your code. Do you think the robot can make the sandwich based off of your instructions? Are there steps you missed? Are there steps you don't need? Are the steps in the right order? Fix the bugs in your code!

Review your code again. Continue fixing it until the robot can make the perfect sandwich. Yum!

automate: To run or operate using machines instead of people.

code: The instructions a computer programmer writes in a programming language to tell a computer what to do.

energy: Usable power.

GPS: Short for Global Positioning System, a navigation system that uses satellite signals to determine location.

graphics: Pictures on a computer screen.

GUI: Short for Graphical User Interface, a program that allows someone to use icons or other visual indicators to interact with the device.

HTML: Short for Hypertext Markup Language, a popular programming language for making web pages.

Java: A popular programming language capable of producing software for many different platforms.

mobile applications: Software that run on easy-to-move devices, such as smartphones or tablet computers.

programming languages: Computer languages that tell a computer or machine what to do. Each language has certain strengths, but many can be used to make the same program.

software programs: Written programs or procedures that run on a computer and accomplish certain functions.

```
<!DOCTYPE html>
<html>
    <head>
            <meta charset="utf-8">
            <title>Reg CSS</title>
    </head>
    <body>
        <div class="afr1">
              <div class="afr2"></div>
              <div class="afr3">
                    <div class="afr4"></div>
```

INDEX

TO LEARN MORE

Finding more information is as easy as 1, 2, 3.

① Go to www.factsurfer.com

② Enter "computerprogrammer" into the search box.

③ Click the "Surf" button to see a list of websites.

FACT SURFER